LUDWIG VAN BEETHOVEN

QUARTET

for 2 Violins, Viola and Violoncello
B♭ major/B-Dur/Si♭ majeur
Op. 130

Edited by/Herausgegeben von
Wilhelm Altmann

T0081299

Ernst Eulenburg Ltd

London · Mainz · Madrid · New York · Paris · Tokyo · Toronto · Zürich

BEETHOVEN, OP. 130:
STRING QUARTET IN B FLAT MAJOR.

The B flat major quartet, op. 130, belongs to the three works in this form which Beethoven, as early as January 1823, had intended for Prince Nicholas von Galitzin. But it was only on completion of the A minor quartet in August 1825 that he turned his attention to the present work in B flat major, sketches for which were already in being by the month of March. In a letter to his nephew, dated August 24th 1825, Beethoven expresses the hope of finishing this quartet — the third destined for Prince Galitzin — in ten or twelve days, at the outside. But the year 1826 had arrived before that hope was realised.

The work was performed for the first time by the Schuppanzigh Quartet on March 21st, 1826. Whilst the second movement (Presto) and the fourth (Alla danza tedesca)[1] had to be repeated, the final Fuge — published separately, later on, as op. 133 — failed in its effect. For this reason Beethoven found it necessary to write a new last movement; so after having rejected one outline (Nottebohm, "Neue Beethoviana" 524), in September 1826 he produced the new Finale, for which, on November 25th, his publisher paid him an extra fee of 15 ducats. This easy-flowing finale, reminiscent of Beethoven's youthful manner, was the master's last fully completed composition, after which he only worked at sketches for a quintet.

The firms of Schlesinger (Berlin) and Peters (Leipzig) applied for the publication of the quartet; the suggestion made by Peters, that the work should be submitted on approval, was curtly refused by Beethoven. The publication finally fell to Artaria, of Vienna, who printed this B flat major quartet before Schlesinger did the one in A minor; consequently, the latter work was given a later opus number.

As regards the original manuscript, the first movement and the Cavatina (formerly in the possession of the Mendelssohn-Bartholdy family) together with the Finale (presented by Prof. R. Wagener) are now the property of the Royal Library in Berlin.

The title of the original edition, which appeared after Beethoven's death on May 7th 1827, runs as follows: Troisième Quatuor pour 2 Violons, Alto & Violoncelle, des Quatuors composés et dediés A Son Altesse Monseigneur le Prince Nicolas de Galitzin, Lieutenant Colonel de la Garde de Sa Majesté Imperle de toutes les Russies par Louis van Beethoven, Oeuvre 130. Propriété de l'Editeur. Vienne chez Maths Artaria etc. List number of Score 870, of Parts 871.

All editions of this quartet are distinguished for thorough accuracy; in the original edition and numerous re-prints (except the one by Joachim Moser) only one error is to be noted — in the „Alla danza tedesca" (page 26, II, 4 of the present score) the third quaver in the viola part is wrongly written g instead of b; this is a mistake first pointed out by Dugge.

Wilh. Altmann

---

[1] As Nottebohm has pointed out in "Beethoviana" (1872) p. 53, this movement originally belonged to the A minor quartet and was written in the key of A major.

BEETHOVEN, OP. 130: STREICHQUARTETT

Das B-dur-Quartett op. 130 gehört zu den 3 Werken dieser Gattung, die Beethoven bereits im Januar 1823 dem Fürsten Galitzin zugesagt hatte. Aber erst nachdem er im August 1825 das in a-moll vollendet, machte er sich an das B-dur, für das seit März bereits Skizzen da waren. In einem Briefe an seinen Neffen vom 24. August 1825 spricht er die Hoffnung aus, daß er dieses dritte, für Galitzin bestimmte Quartett in 10, höchstens 12 Tagen vollendet haben würde. Aber es kam wohl das Jahr 1826 heran, ehe es soweit war.

Zur ersten Aufführung gelangte es durch die Quartettgesellschaft Schuppanzigh am 21. März 1826. Während der 2. Satz (Presto) und der 4. (Alla danza tedesca)[1] wiederholt werden mußten, mißfiel die später einzeln als op. 133 veröffentlichte Schlußfuge. Beethoven sah sich daher veranlaßt, einen neuen Schlußsatz zu komponieren; nachdem er einen ersten Entwurf (Nottebohm, „Neue Beethoviana" 524) wieder verworfen hatte, entstand von September 1826 ab das neue Finale, für das ihm der Verleger am 25. November ein Extrahonorar von 15 Dukaten zahlte. Es ist dieses leichtflüssige, auf Beethovens Jugendstil hindeutende Finale seine letzte wirklich ausgeführte Komposition, nach der er nur noch an Skizzen zu einem Quintett gearbeitet hat.

Um den Verlag hatten sich Schlesinger-Berlin und Peters-Leipzig beworben; das Ansinnen des letzteren, ihm das Quartett zur Ansicht zu senden, wies Beethoven kurz zurück. Den Verlag erhielt schließlich Artaria-Wien, der dieses B-dur-Quartett eher druckte als Schlesinger das in a-moll; dieses bekam infolgedessen eine spätere Opuszahl.

Von dem Manuskript befinden sich der erste Satz und die Kavatine (früher im Besitze der Familie von Mendelssohn-Bartholdy) sowie das Finale (geschenkt von Prof. R. Wagener) im Besitz der Königl. Bibliothek zu Berlin.

Der Titel der Original-Ausgabe, die nach Beethovens Tod am 7. Mai 1827 erschienen ist, lautet: Troisième Quatuor pour 2 Violons, Alto & Violoncelle des Quatuors composés et dediés A Son Altesse Monseigneur le Prince Nicolas de Galitzin, Lieutenant Colonel de la Garde de Sa Majesté Imperle de toutes les Russies par Louis van Beethoven. Oeuvre 130. Propriété de l'Editeur. Vienne chez Maths Artaria etc. Verlags-No. der Partitur 870, der Stimmen 871.

Alle Drucke dieses Quartetts zeichnen sich durch große Korrektheit aus; in der Original-Ausgabe und zahlreichen Nachdrucken (jedoch nicht bei Joachim Moser) steht nur in „Alla danza tedesca" (S. 26, II, 4 unserer Partitur) im 3. Achtel der Viola fälschlich g statt h, ein Fehler, auf den zuerst Dugge aufmerksam gemacht hat.

Wilh. Altmann

---

[1] Wie Nottebohm „Beethoviana" (1872) S. 53 nachgewiesen hat, gehörte dieser Satz ursprünglich in das a-moll-Quartett und stand daher auch ursprünglich in A-dur.

Quartet

I

L. van Beethoven, Op. 130
1770-1827

　　E E. 1109　　Ernst Eulenburg Ltd
Ernst Eulenburg Ltd

2

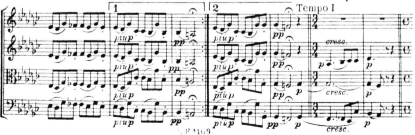

6

II

L'istesso tempo

E. E. 1109

III

Andante con moto, ma non troppo

poco scherzando

E 1109

Tempo I

70

80

IV

Alla danza tedesca

Allegro assai

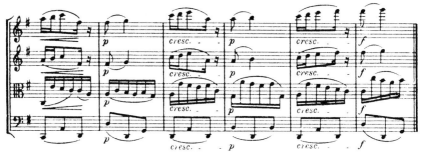

Cavatina
Adagio molto espressivo
V

E.E.1109

60

Finale Allegro

VI

10

E. E. 1169

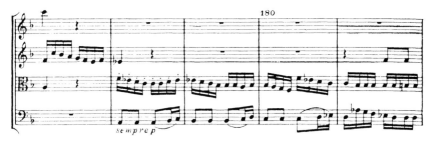

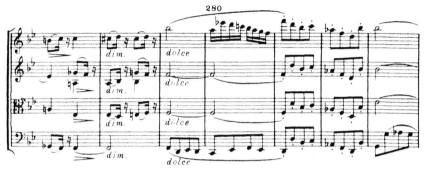

390

400

410

E.E.1109

E E 1109